Books & Things Publishing LLC, Chantilly, VA
First published in the United States of America
by Books & Things Publishing, 2023

First edition published 2023

Text copyright 2023 Danielle Marietta & Marissa Kearney

Illustration copyright 2023 Ryan Odagawa for 5Rings Studio

Story & Production Consulting - Savv Media

Books & Things Publishing supports copyright and
its protection of diverse authors who create inclusive books.

ISBN: 978-1-962140-90-4 (HARDCOVER)
ISBN: 978-1-7357218-9-7 (PAPERBACK)
ISBN: 978-1-962140-89-8 (eBOOK)

Library of Congress Control Number: 2023917972

Designed and formatted by Enzo Varrie

This book is a work of fiction. All rights reserved, including the right of reproduction in whole or in part in any form.

Books & Things Publishing, LLC
4410 Brookfield Corporate Dr. #220149
Chantilly, VA 20153

For more information on author events or bulk orders,
please visit us online at www.booksandthingspublishing.com

Help support by leaving reviews on all platforms.

Visit the author websites and sign up for their newsletters.

Marissa Kearney www.retailwhileblack.shop

Danielle Marietta www.daniellemariettabooks.com

Dedication Page

"Flossy, Glossy, Diamonds and Pearls.
Candy, Suga, and Cavities fo' sure."

For my kids, Ty and Lina, who keep me silly.
-Marissa

For Dillon, Trevor and Taylin,
Never stop believing in the magic within yourself.
-Danielle

About the Authors

Marissa Kearney is a former teacher and award-winning content creator focused on social activism, education and the discovery of Black-owned brands and representation on the retail shelves. Her platforms have helped numerous brands and authors start a successful retail journey, promote brand awareness and increase revenue. As a result, these businesses have scaled to stores across the US. Now it is her turn to add a piece of representation to the retail shelves.

Danielle Marietta is the owner and founder of Books & Things Publishing. She is the award-winning author of Mr. Maloof, The Holly-day After and Bubble Sea. She studied journalism at Howard University but didn't find her true voice in writing until she became a mother. Danielle is inspired daily by her children and writes for them and all who are looking for a little imaginative fun. Now with her publishing company, Danielle hopes to uplift the voices of the underrepresented and continue to diversify bookshelves globally.

Table of Contents

CHAPTER 1
The Lost Tooth 1

CHAPTER 2
The Trap. 7

CHAPTER 3
Tooth Fair-He 19

CHAPTER 4
Welcome to Root Canal 27

CHAPTER 5
Undercover Fair-He 45

CHAPTER 6
Tooth Jewelry 57

CHAPTER 7
The Truth Behind the Tooth 67

CHAPTER 8
The Chase. 73

CHAPTER 9
The Return 79

CHAPTER 10
Back to Reality...Maybe 89

CHAPTER I

THE LOST TOOTH

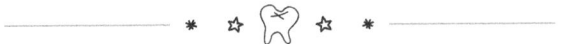

Everything goes down in the lunchroom.

That's the one place teachers aren't looking over our shoulders and where we have the freedom to just be kids. It's where I made real friendships my first week at school after bonding over matching kicks. The lunchroom is a true test to see who's fly and who's...almost fly. Anything that is going to happen happens in that 30-minute window of a kid's day. And today at lunch, I bit into an apple and when I pulled it out of my mouth, my loose tooth was still

lodged in it. I held that apple up to the sky like the ultimate trophy it was.

"Don't lose it. If you want that money, you'd better put it away until you get home," Kaylee mumbled while taking another bite of her mystery meat patty. Does anyone really know what it is? I'm pretty sure it's the same mystery meat my parents talk about when going down their middle school memory lane.

"She's right," Milo said. "My last tooth got me five bucks."

"Five bucks?! No way. You must have one of those good fairies. I'm lucky if I get a quarter. Ain't that right, Gabe?" she asked me, looking for someone to back her up.

"Uh, yeah, sure. I mean I usually get a dollar or two," I told them, not wanting to make anyone feel bad for getting a little less.

At that same moment, the Big Boys passed by our table and the leader of their group snatched the apple right out of my hand. I stood right up with my chest puffed out like I was actually about to do something. In reality, I instantly regretted getting up, but it was too late.

"It doesn't even matter. Y'all know the tooth fairy isn't real. It's just some made up hoax by a bunch of dentists hoping to get kids to brush their teeth." They all laughed and tossed the apple around me and back at my tray. They brushed past my now-deflated chest and headed out of the cafeteria.

"Shoot! Where is it, where is it?" I mumbled as I lifted up my tray. The tooth had popped out of the apple when it was tossed back. "That was close," I said when I saw it wedged between my chocolate milk and two-month-old crusty burger bun.

Kaylee took another bite. "What a bunch of jerks. All I know, Gabe, is if someone is leaving any amount of money for my dirty old teeth, I'll keep putting it under my pillow." We all nodded in agreement. We are all at that age, as my mom would say, where these tales we have grown up hearing are sounding a bit too magical for reality, but like Kaylee said, if putting a tooth under my pillow gets me cash money, who am I to argue?

I put the tiny tooth up to my eye to take a closer look and admire its shine. Then I stuff it in my sandwich bag for safekeeping.

Time seemed to move in slow motion for the rest of the day. Every few minutes, I'd pat my pocket to make sure the tooth was still there.

When the school day finally ended and the B.O. filled bus finally stopped on my street, I squeezed out the double doors before they were fully opened. I ran from the moment my feet touched the pavement!

I went up the stairs in our building, skipping every other step as I went. As I pushed open the door, I blurted out the news before my dad could even say hello.

CHAPTER 2

THE TRAP

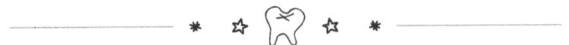

"My tooth came out at lunch today!" I ripped the used sandwich bag from my pocket and held it out. My dad smiled, walked over and rubbed the top of my head while reminding me to put my tooth under my pillow so the tooth fairy could get it. As he turned to finish his work for the day, a question flooded my brain and I had to ask.

"Hey dad," I mumbled completely awkwardly. "Do you believe in the tooth fairy?"

The keys on his computer stopped clicking and he paused. "Yeah, don't you?"

Play it cool Gabe, I thought to myself. "I mean, it does seem kind of babyish," I said with a shrug and started pacing around with both hands shoved deep into my pockets. "I mean, has anyone ever seen her? What does she look like?" My feet stopped and I looked right at my dad. "What in the world does the tooth fairy do with all those teeth?" I walked over to dad's desk and slapped both hands down like this was some kind of courtroom and I was pleading my case. "You ever thought about that? What if some old weirdo is hiding out on a mountain of kid's teeth?" I shuddered at the thought, but the more questions I said out loud, the more questions I had. "What if ..."

Dad had a puzzled look before turning fully to face me and saying, "Whoa, man, slow down! You're asking a lot of questions."

"Well?" I said, lifting my hands up and shrugging while still waiting for my answers.

Dad sighed, "She takes them back to her magical land of teeth." We stared at each other. "Obviously." He raised his eyebrows, but neither one of us was convinced. His delivery truly was all wrong.

But somehow, thinking he was in the clear, my dad turned back to his computer and started to type again. He should really know me better by now, I thought. Then I doubled down, "Okay, then what?"

"I don't know champ! You'll have to ask her!" he sighed without missing a single moment on his keyboard. I knew this tone all too well. I had maxed out questions for the day.

Reading the vibe, I headed down the hall and into my room, questions still bouncing around in my head. How was I supposed to ask her when I would be sleeping?! Unless...I had an idea!

"Dad," I yelled. "Will you help me trap the tooth fairy so I can ask her myself, you know, like you suggested?"

I could hear his mumbled laugh from the other end of the house. "Of course!" I knew I could count on my dad! He was always down for anything, and I loved that about him.

"All right," he said and I heard his his heavy steps walking my way. "What's the plan?"

* * *

"This has to be the dumbest idea I've ever heard," my older sister, Tay, said after hearing my plan. We all sat around the dinner table, quiet after all my ideas were shot down by my good ol' sis who rarely leaves her room unless it's to see her friends, eat or go to school.

"I don't see you dropping any ideas," I huffed.

"I don't know G, but why the tooth fairy? Why not set the bar higher and go after the big man himself?" she said.

"Santa?! It's October!"

"Whatever," she mumbled. "Good luck with your mission Mr. 007. I'm heading out to get some new shoes with the girls."

"Hater." I said to her back as she walked her plate into the kitchen.

After brainstorming over my second massive bowl of mom's famous spaghetti and meatballs, dad and I got to work. This was going to be the best tooth fairy trapping device ever. Figuring out what size

to make it was tricky. She has to be small to be able to get under pillows without anyone feeling her. Oh, and she is a fairy. You know, with magic! I wasn't sure what to do with that bit of information, but it was worth mentioning.

We decided an old glass salt shaker would be best. We would be able to see her inside and hopefully block her magic! I took some of my dad's fishing string and tied a tiny loop around the rim of the shaker and then a bigger circle around the entire trap. We tucked it all under my pillow and it seemed great, but I knew something was missing.

"What's wrong Gabe? You don't think it will work?" Dad asked, sensing my hesitation.

"Nope, something isn't right." I reached over to my desk and grabbed the duct tape. "We need to

make sure there is only one way in," I told dad as I taped my pillow to my bed. "This won't work if she has four different entries and exits."

"Smart kid," dad mumbled.

"There. Perfect." I took an old bell from my kiddie bike and attached it to the string, so when it moved, the ding would wake me up. We both stood with our arms crossed and looked at what we had created.

"It's actually pretty good," he said.

"You sound surprised," I smirked up at him.

I carefully climbed in, making sure not to detach anything on the trap. After trying to get comfortable, I figured I should sleep on the floor instead. So I rolled onto the floor and looked up at my ceiling. Then it dawned on me that the tooth fairy might look under this wadded up sweatshirt I was using for a pillow and miss my tooth and the actual trap on my bed. Relocation number two, back onto my bed. My dad just rolled his eyes.

"All right now. I think that's it. Night bud," dad said as he turned off the light and started to close the door.

"Well, hang on now. Let me check this trap out," my mom said as she came in. She inspected the duct tape chaos that was my pillow and kissed my forehead. "Looks good, Gabe. Good luck tonight," she said as she pulled the sheet up high under my chin, just how I like it.

"Ouch," I said as her ring scratched my cheek. "Every time, Mom?!"

"Sorry sweetie, this old ring is getting loose. I need to get these pieces that hold the stone pushed back into place," she said as she fidgeted and spun her ring around her finger. "Are you ok?"

"Yeah, no biggie Mom. Love you."

"Love ya baby." She kissed my forehead and headed out of my room, closing the door behind her.

I laid there looking up at the shadows created from my pile of laundry on my desk chair. I'm grown now, but that shadow still looks suspicious. Trying to refocus my thoughts, I tried to imagine what this fairy chick was really going to look like. I couldn't wait to ask her about everything. Was she really some weirdo hoarding a bunch of teeth? And if so,

why teeth and not...I don't know, hair or fingernail clippings? Eww. Well, what if I catch her and she only speaks French? I don't know French! But on the flip side, maybe she will know the big man himself, Santa!

My mind was racing with all the possibilities and a little doubt, too. Haven't other kids tried this before? It's not going to work. If the tooth fairy really is magic, she will magic herself out, glass container or not. But, and this was a big but, what if it does work? Soon enough, between one of my millions of thoughts, I drift off to sleep and those thoughts become dreams.

CHAPTER 3

TOOTH FAIR-HE

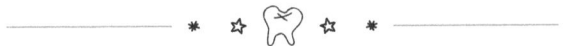

KURFLUMP! SNAP! RING!

"What the!" I shot up out of my sleep. Wait...Did I do it?! Did I trap the tooth fairy? I ripped the duct tape off the edges of the pillow and as I slowly lifted it up, a warm glowing light shined from inside the trap.

"No. Freaking. Way!" As the pillow lifted higher, my eyes grew wider. This is NOT what I was expecting. Not even close!

The sneakers were the coolest I'd ever seen and the first thing I noticed as the glow slowly faded. Then he smiled at me and his teeth shined almost as bright as the sun. No, brighter! And the cut. My guy had a fresh haircut, a tight lineup and a tooth symbol on the side. It reminded me of the lightning bolt my Uncle Kenny tried to give me that one time. Let's just say I never went back to him for a cut.

But hold up, how did I miss this? He is a he! He can't be the tooth fairy! No way!

I snatched up the salt shaker and rapidly fired questions at the unsuspecting little man that may or

may not have been the tooth fairy. That was clearly still up for debate!

"Who are you? How did you get here? How'd you get in there? Did you fly? Are you really the tooth fairy?" I asked without taking a single breath.

"Whoa there, Gabe! You can't just trap me and shake me down for all my family secrets!" he exclaimed.

"What happens to the teeth? Where do you live? Where do you put the teeth after you collect them? Are you some kinda weirdo? Are you really...her?"

"Her who? I am he, the air fair-he, or tooth fair-he if you want to get all politically correct," he frustratedly dropped his arms and started pacing the tiny two steps forward and back in the salt shaker. "They always get that wrong. I hate when people mess up my name. Y'all just say it too fast. You do everything too fast. Ya eat too fast, brush too fast, say fair-he too fast." His glow was back and stronger now the more upset he got.

"Oh, but please!" my mouth whistled. "I gotta know! Help a nerdy kid get a little street cred in the lunchroom. Please, oh please, help a kid out," I cried.

The look this little man was giving me made me think he was going to say no, but he didn't. Instead, he smiled brightly and said, "All right kid, chill. You know, Santa..... He warned me about you. He said you are a smart kid who loves adventures!"

Not wanting to blink, fearing that would be the moment he would disappear and this all would be over, I just stared at him full of hope. He winked and took a deep sigh. I crept a little closer, nearly holding my breath, my nose touching the glass that stood between us.

"Here's the thing, kid. Technically, I'm not allowed to tell you." He paused. I sunk deeper into my bed and my smile quickly went away. "Geez kid. You really know how to break a guy down. Look, I might not be able to tell you," he paused. "But no one said I can't show you." His eyes dazzled. "I'll need a little help first."

"Oh yeah, anything!" I said a little too loud and way overly excited.

He motioned for me to lift up the trap. "You can start by letting me out. I could do it myself, but I'm not trying to show you all my tricks on day one. We just met and all. You understand."

"Sorry about that," I said, as I carefully tilted the shaker back, careful not to hit him and let him out.

"I'll also need that tooth of yours. Inventory is running low." He reached out and picked up my tooth that had looked huge next to him. Except soon as he touched it, it instantly shrunk. It became about the size of one of his tiny teeth and could much more easily fit into his bag. "Ok, so I've only seen this in the movies and never done it myself."

"Wait, what do you mean?" I started getting nervous for whatever was about to happen.

"Just. Dont. Blink!" With a snap of his fingers, my tooth turned into metallic dust and a light shot out so bright, I had to close my eyes. Not a second later, I opened my eyes and found I was in...I think, his backpack. It was dark and full of glitter and sand. It felt like I was trying to stay above quicksand. "Hold on tight, little man," he said. I pulled myself up and flung my arms over the edge of the zipper that had been left open just enough that I could fit out. He was huge! Or was I tiny?

I looked down and realized we had gotten outside and were flying over my neighborhood. I saw my house getting smaller and smaller as we drifted away. There's that little store on the corner that my crew and I meet at every day on our walk to school. Looking back, I saw the smallest burst of energy shoot out from his kicks and he said, "Under the big dipper and over the moon, hold on tight, we'll be there soon!"

CHAPTER 4

WELCOME TO ROOT CANAL

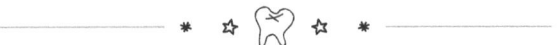

We flew up, up and up. So high, and it was so cool. But it was a little hard to tell if I was excited or about to pee my pants. At this point, it was pretty 50/50.

"Air Fair-He 10 to Mother Earth. I am ready to return," he said into his watch.

MOTHER EARTH IS IN ON THIS, I thought wildly to myself. How big is this operation?

As we peaked over the moon, I noticed the stars, or what I thought were stars, shift into a new pattern in the sky. They moved like a lock as they all shifted into place. Watching closely as they turned in the sky, they reminded me oddly of my cousin Tommy's braces. "Oh, I get it!"

The tooth fair-he looked down at me and smiled, his superhero fist out in front of himself guiding the way towards the moving stars. When we both looked back up, a light came into view right between the two front teeth. Front teeth of the stars, that is. Like an opening, or a portal to another world, we flew directly through that giant gap between the two front teeth of the stars and I couldn't believe my eyes.

"What the heck is this, Never Never Land or something?" We were flying over what looked like a giant floating island shaped like a tooth. It was some kind of toothy kingdom.

Hills of blue fluffy mountains stretched as far as the eyes could see and in the middle of it all stood a pearly white castle with an enormous river flowing through the silver metal gates.

As we continued to get closer, I noticed the river was not flowing with water, but instead with some kind of glittery, sand substance. Come to think of

it, it was just like the stuff I was sitting in in the fairy's, wait, fair-he's backpack.

"Wait, is this what happens to all the teeth?" I yelled out to the tooth fair-he and pointed down.

"Yep!"

"No cap?"

"No cap! Welcome to Root Canal. This is where the tooth fair-hes from all over the world drop their teeth after collecting them," he said through another dazzling smile. "Back in the day it was filled with literal teeth. It got a little weird so we had to upgrade. This is much better all around. It's how the teeth get…" he paused to find the right word, "sorted."

"Sorted? Like in Harry Potter?" I asked excitedly.

"Kind of," he answered, "except we don't use a hat. That kind of magic is foolishness. Look to your left kid. We use the Whirlpool of Wisdom."

I looked over my shoulder and saw the dust spinning up, like an upside-down tornado. At the top, beautiful glowing glitter went over one mountain, and dull-looking sand went over another smaller mountain. It seemed to be putting the pretty glitter on one side and the not so pretty on the other. I still wasn't sure what it meant, but we flew by too quickly for me to get another word out.

Soaring low, just over the Root Canal, we stopped and floated in place as a giant iron gate lifted up, allowing us to pass through. I tried to take that moment and look around to memorize everything I was seeing. We followed the path of the canal into the pearly white castle. When the tunnel opened up, we slowed down and the tooth fair-he pulled me out of his backpack. As we landed, he set me on the ground and as soon as my feet touched, I grew in size. Talk about a crazy feeling! It's like when my mom makes me eat my great aunt's potato salad, ugh. I'm a texture guy. But I grew to be almost as big as he was. I stretched out and checked to make sure I was all here.

I looked up to see we had stopped under the shade of something like a tree. It was shaped just like a tree, but what should have been leaves looked more like clouds. Colorful clouds.

"Look, but don't touch. Cotton candy." He nodded up. "Looks good, but I promise you, the more of it you eat, the worse off your teeth will be." Mom always says that. Maybe she did know what she was talking about.

"Here, I always have an extra pair of Air Fair-Hes on me, just in case. Can't cruise around in busted kicks. Put these on and everyone will think you are one of us," he said.

I grabbed the red and black shoes with little wings on the side and sat down to put them on. When I did, a new, weird, tingling feeling made me crinkle my nose and POOF. Wings shot out from the top of my back! I spun around in a circle repeatedly trying to catch a glimpse of them, like a dog after his tail.

"WOW! No way! I can fly?"

"No, you only look like you can fly. They only work for real fair-hes. Don't go and try jumping off anything. I do not want to explain to your parents how you went from Gabe to pancake," he chuckled loudly at his joke and the look it brought to my face.

We walked a bit, staying by the edge of the canal until we made our way past the giant castle doors that looked like they led to the main center of the castle.

The canal twisted and turned and I was mesmerized watching it. The way the cotton candy trees lined the canal reminded me of the chocolate factory from the old Willy Wonka story. Up ahead, I could see that it flowed into a swirling fountain of dust with beautiful colors. Sparkling silvers, golds, iridescent purples, pinks and blues all bubbling up and pouring over the top edge of the fountain. My friends will never believe this, I thought.

"Hey kid, watch this," he said as he placed me on an actual cloud for a few seconds. Yeah, a cloud. I guess because we are in the sky, they just float around wherever? I'll go with that.

"I can't believe you have moving clouds for seats when we just have hard metal benches at home. This is way better already," I said.

"Out of everything you've seen so far, that's what's way better? Have you not been looking around?" He said sarcastically, flailing his arms around. The tooth fair-he spun his backpack around to his front and mumbled to himself as he poured it all into his hand. All of the dust and glitter from his bag formed into a ball as it spilled out. He swung his backpack back around and held out his hand with the dust ball floating just above his palm. It looked exactly like my basketball at home except, you know, made of glitter.

"Is that tooth dust?" I was a little worried about what the answer would be, but couldn't not ask.

"Shh," he told me as he aimed, spun his hands, then threw the dust while holding his stance like he just shot a game winning buzzer beater.

"KOBE," he yelled as the ball hit the center of the whirlpool and glowed brightly for a second, before turning into shimmering golden dust.

"Wow, Gabe. You had an excellent tooth. Only the best teeth turn into gold dust!"

"Does this mean I am rich? Because there is a new PlayStation with my name all over it!"

"No," he laughed. "But it does fetch a pretty penny. Have you ever put a tooth under your pillow and found that you get different amounts of money from time to time?"

I paused, "Actually, yes! That has happened to me. And my friends and I all get different amounts, too."

"Yeah, it kind of depends on a few things. First off, your first tooth loss is usually a big deal. We all get excited visiting a kid for the first time. Typically, that gets you a bit more than the rest. The cleanest teeth can run you more, too," the tooth fair-he explained. "But then a few other conditions determine how much you really get."

I just stared at him and wanted him to keep talking. This was it, all the things I had ever wondered. And here I was, sitting on some cloud learning the actual truth behind the tooth mystery from the tooth fair-he himself.

"But don't get me started on the times we don't or can't pick up the teeth at all. I'd hate to see that kid's face in the morning." He took a moment. "I've only missed one pickup and I don't plan on doing it again!"

Missing a pick up? Like that time I left my tooth under the pillow but it was still there the next morning with no money in its place? I thought, but before I could question any further, other tooth fair-hes caught my eye. Had they been flying around the entire time and I hadn't noticed? I tried to focus and noticed they were all flying around in similar gear to what my tooth fair-he was wearing. Some outfits were a bit different, but they all had one thing in common, their shoes.

"How many are there?" I asked and pointed up to the others.

"Thousands!" he said quickly. "Well, thousands of fair-hes. You can also become a mouthguard or a tooth jewel-her. That's who is handling all these canals. The tooth jewel-hers really get to flex their magic," he said.

"TOOTH JEWEL-HER?" I shouted. This operation is way more complicated than I thought. Mother Earth, Santa, mouthguards, jewel-hers? Now I had follow-up questions to my original questions. What the heck is a tooth jewel-her and what do they do?

He reached down to his shiny silver watch and turned its face twice. Light shot out from the center, and we were zooming through the castle and past other fair-hes. Eventually, we came to a stop and I could see we were in a hallway with rooms on the left and the right.

POP!

We arrived with a quick drop to the ground. I fell on my butt but this guy hit the superhero landing.

Sweet, I thought. Then he gave me a wink when he saw me looking. Jerk, I thought next. Getting up off the floor, we found ourselves in a giant room with a tooth-shaped chandelier, marble floors, and trolleys full of that same tooth dust I had seen just moments ago.

CHAPTER 5

UNDERCOVER FAIR-HE

On one side of the room were three trolleys, each one with a cloud of different colored dust from the canal. On the other side of the room, there was only one trolley, and it was full of purplish black tooth dust. It looked kind of gross, if you ask me.

"Quick, over here," the tooth fair-he said as he nudged me down a hallway. He opened a door with a sign on the front that said Janitor. "There's one thing I forgot to mention."

Oh no. The look on his face was freaking me out. He had seemed so calm and chill about everything up until this moment. I wanted to say something, but a roll of paper towels fell off the shelf and startled me.

"Look kid, put this jacket on to blend in because you really aren't supposed to be here."

"Yeah, no kidding! If everyone knew this place existed, we'd have been catching tooth fairy -uh, fair-hes, for years! I can't wait to tell everyone at lunch tomorrow!"

"Listen, that's the thing. There won't be a tomorrow if we get caught," he mumbled as he checked behind him to make sure the door was shut.

"WHAT?!

"What does that mean?!" I yelled hysterically. "I'm too young to die. I have my whole life ahead of me. I haven't even finished middle school yet! Wait, I haven't even truly started!" I was starting to panic and dropped to the floor. "Why did you even bring me here if it's that dangerous?"

In that second, the door handle began to rattle and before I could fully panic, the door creaked open. I hopped up as fast as I could and stood right behind…wait, how do I not know his name? Is it just tooth fair-he?

"Hey Gemma, Jade and Diamond! How's it shinin'?" he said and flashed his money maker smile. Clearly he thought he was acting normal, but I don't even know him like that and could tell it wasn't even close to anyone's normal.

They were standing right outside of the janitor's closet. The three of them, looking at the two of us. Silence. I eyed them quickly and noticed that each one had their own style and all were decked out in jewels. These must be the tooth jewel-hers!

* * *

Gemma was wearing a blue tracksuit, Air Fair-He sneakers, box braids, and a giant letter G draped over three other necklaces. That's why I guessed she was Gemma. Jade had a loud pink curly fro, big diamond hoop earrings, a green flowy dress, and bracelets going up each arm. And Diamond – well she was shining the brightest! She didn't wear other stones, nope, not her. Only diamonds on Diamond. Her suit and high top mohawk were so glittery it was hard to look at her for too long without bringing my hand up to shield my eyes.

"Hey Tony?!" They said in unison.

His name is Tony?! I guess having everyone named "Tooth Fair-He" would be pretty confusing.

"Tony?" I quietly questioned while he tried to cough over my words. But it wasn't enough.

They all locked their eyes locked on mine at the same time and they immediately looked panicked. Welp. The wings were clearly a terrible disguise. These people did magic. Did I think I was going to fool them with faux wings and the anime pj's my grandma got me last Christmas that were a bit too small and showed off my slightly ashy ankles and full borrowed shoes? This is bad.

"YOU BROUGHT A CHILD IN? ARE YOU OUT OF YOUR MOLARS?" Jade yelled.

They have to stop with the tooth words, I thought, trying not to roll my eyes. My mom wasn't here but she would not like me to be rude, especially when I was already on the road to trouble. I reminded myself to try and 'fix my face' before anyone caught me mid eye roll.

"Relax, I haven't broken any rules," Tony said smoothly. "The kid trapped me and had questions. Isn't it better to educate the kids instead of treating them like babies? They're the future. Besides, he only wants to see what happens to the teeth. We won't touch anything." He looked at me and winked while mouthing "don't touch anything."

They were not convinced. They stood for some time with their eyes as round as basketballs before Gemma spoke again. "If the Grand Fair-He catches you, we never saw you and you never saw us. Swear on your molars!" they rapped, forming a circle around Tony and pointing their fingers at his head. "Swear!" He said with his hands up.

Oh no! Are they going to magic his head off? I have to help him and do something.

"I swear!" Tony and I say in unison. He looks over at me, then back at the trio in front of us. "Look, this kid fully built a trap and caught me. He's not messing around. Let's show the kid how the real magic happens," Tony said with another wink, and he grabbed my hand.

This was it. It was really happening! I couldn't believe it.

"Well, would you guys stop hiding in the janitor's closet and try looking less like you are guilty and more like you are exactly where you are supposed to be?" Gemma stated.

The three jewel-hers all turned their watch faces like Tony had earlier and started to shimmer.

Then, all at once, the five of us poof'd from the closet into an empty trolley directly behind the one full of gross purplish black dust. Without any

help, one by one all of the trolleys connected into a magical train. I hope this thing has brakes, I thought to myself as we launched down an empty hallway.

Two seconds into the ride and I realized I should have been more worried about having a seatbelt. The pearly white hallways bent in a million directions with steep drops, tight twists, and loop-de-loops. In these brief moments, it felt like we had traveled a hundred miles just to get from one side of the castle to the other. The walls blurred around us as the jewel-hers all chatted away happily.

Meanwhile, I was trying to keep my eyes open against the force of the wind. Why was I crying? Well, not crying, but this wind was making my eyes water. I saw Tony looking at me and I made a note to tell my mom I didn't want to go to Universal Studios after all. I was definitely going to be sick. This trolley-turned-roller-coaster ride seemed to go on forever and was not my thing. Just when I thought I would lose my dinner, we came to an abrupt stop in front of a giant shiny door.

"Thank goodness," I mumbled.

"All right, this is us. Come on, Mr. Curious," Jade said as we hopped out of the trolley. It could have just been my imagination, but Tony seemed very amused that I was going to puke at any moment. Did he know it was going to be a high-speed roller coaster? Of course, he did. I was starting to not feel so bad that I had trapped him in that salt shaker after all. Punishment for us both.

Suddenly, the giant silver door in front of us sprung open and revealed a room full of wonder.

CHAPTER 6
TOOTH JEWELRY

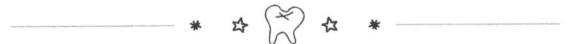

The room itself was the brightest of bright whites, but everything inside was so colorful. Big machines with different conveyor belts wound back and forth and the humming sounds of them all made a pretty sick beat. Looking around I could tell I wasn't the only one that thought so. Jewel-hers were walking around -- all to the main beat drumming on. I could tell they were all jewel-hers because they were all decked out in different stones. Even the jewel-hers standing by the belts checking objects as they went by had a slight shoulder or

head bob going. I couldn't quite tell what they were doing or looking at, but as I took a step closer...wait, was that the tooth dust?! I paused to slow down my racing thoughts and I really didn't want to jump to conclusions, but I'm pretty sure now, it's the same glitter sand from the wisdom whirlpool or whirlpool of wisdom...whatever Tony called it. It looked like the machines first sorted the glitter dust by color. As the dust got sucked into glass tubes, you could see it spinning around frantically. When it disappeared from sight, levers began twitching and pumps began pumping. Different knobs began turning, slowly at first, then faster and faster. Each machine grew a little louder as buzzers went off when whatever was happening inside was done. Then, bloop, bloop, bloop. Beautiful stones appeared in a single file line onto the belt. And on the side of each of the belts stood the bopping lady jewelers. Well, jewel-hers.

One machine that took in the pinkish-red glitter was spitting out rubies. The purple machine that was sucking in all the same-colored dust was dropping amethysts on its belt. Another, dropping emeralds. And the biggest machine at the end of the room filled with gold dust-- I walked closer! Diamonds!

"No freaking way!" I said quietly. Then, as the wheels began turning in my head like the wheels on the giant machines around me, I realized what I was actually seeing.

"You mean to tell me people are wearing kids' teeth around their necks? THAT'S SO GROSS," I shouted in disbelief and ten times louder than I meant to.

The tooth jewel-hers all paused at first, then laughed. Then Gemma spoke, "I bet your winter jacket has wool on it. You didn't think it was weird to wear sheep's hair?"

"Or that you eat baby chickens for breakfast?" Diamond said. Everyone froze and stared. We all had a confused and disgusted look on our faces. "Eggs, people. I'm talking about eggs."

"Ahh..." we all said in unison, followed by an immediate, "Eww."

"Or sauce that a literal insect made, called honey?" Jade sang.

Now that I think about it, the world is a very strange place. Maybe I should have trapped Mother Earth to ask her what the heck she was thinking. Is she even a thing to be trapped?

"The earth is a fragile place, and we have to protect it," Gemma said as she worked her magic. "Teeth are harder than gold, silver, iron, and steel. It makes them the perfect substance for so many things. The problem is kids aren't taking care of their teeth like they used to," she said while lifting her hand up through a pile of the glittery substance and letting it fall between her fingertips. "Once upon a time we had so much beautiful sand to work with; now we have more coal. All our proportions are off."

"Not only that," Tony chimed in. "Kids don't believe in us like they used to. The more kids stop believing, the more of us just disappear." They all took a moment and paused. "I'm missing a lot of good buddies with this generation."

"Well, if you get caught by the Grand Fair-He or don't get this kid out of here before morning, you will be banished, too!" Gemma said.

Banished?! I definitely didn't sign up for all of this. I just wanted to know what happens to the teeth.

Jade saw the panic in my face and tried her best to comfort me. "Look kid, you will be ok. Tony is a good guy."

Gemma jumped in to change the subject. "Here, watch this." She grabbed a ball of dust and made a perfect oval diamond. "We use teeth in lots of ways that give back to the planet. Instead of taking the materials from the earth, our magic makes an exact replica!" Gemma explained.

"Hold still, kid," Diamond said as she tucked the sleeves of my pajamas into the coat. "I don't know how Tony expected you to be disguised in anime jammies."

Tony scowled and started walking around the room with the jewel-hers in tow, telling me what each machine did.

One machine was almost exactly like my big sister's favorite beach floaty. It was 100 times as big but shifted the sand left and right moving the sparkly dust into even, small piles on a conveyor belt below.

Jade stopped to inspect the piles and snapped her fingers to shoot the dust into the air. It was beautiful. It looked almost exactly like pictures of the Milky Way in my science book.

All of the jewel-hers floated into the air, grabbing pieces here and there. They looked oddly like an album cover as they moved their fingers in circles, effortlessly forming diamond earrings, rings, and necklaces. After watching for a while, I couldn't help but wonder...

"How does this jewelry get to the store?" I thought out loud. "Like back at home. Down on earth? If this place isn't earth, what is it?!"

"It's not quite earth," Tony started.

CHAPTER 7

THE TRUTH BEHIND THE TOOTH

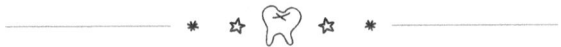

"Part of becoming a human jewel-her on earth is taking a test from the Grand Fair-He himself. Everyone is sworn to secrecy," Gemma said, pointing to a giant portrait hanging high on the wall.

The Grand Fair-He wasn't as old as I thought he would be. In fact, he looked not much older than Tony, but according to the information on the portrait, he was over 3000 years old! He must wear those green face masks like my mom and dad do to stay young.

"Once all the jewelry is made, we pack each item and send them all to the stores using Santa's sleigh. The elves deliver them to each location," Gemma continued.

The shock on my face must have been obvious because Gemma laughed and said, "What did you think the elves did for the other 11 months out of the year when they aren't working for Santa? His sleigh is the only thing fast enough to deliver all over the world in one night." She rolled her eyes and got back to work.

I hope Santa won't be mad at me for trapping my tooth fair-he. I worked really hard to not be on the naughty list this year. I even tried to be nice to my sister when she was being a brat. And that's a daily situation!

All of the lights turned gray as the cart of purplish-gray dust moved into the room and floated to a new set of trolley tracks.

"What is that stuff?" I asked disgustedly.

"This is what happens when you don't take care of your teeth. It turns to unusable coal. Not even the best jewel-her can make jewels out of that stuff," Diamond said with a twinkle of sadness. "No amount of magic can fix an unbrushed and unloved tooth. Sadly, we are getting more and more of it. Almost too much to handle. The fair-he crown is what ultimately is keeping us all here but we need good teeth to keep it powered. The fair-hes are disappearing because the kids don't believe in us and kids are not brushing so we get more of this waste. We just can't keep it powered like we used to. It's only a matter of time."

"A matter of time before what? What happens if it all stops?" I asked.

No one wanted to answer. "We all," Tony paused, "fade. I'm sure you know of a kid or maybe you yourself lost a tooth once and the tooth fair-he didn't come. It's not always because their teeth aren't clean."

"But don't worry kid, there are still a lot of us out here putting in work," Tony reassured me.

"So all this coal dust..."

"Have you ever gotten coal in your stocking or a ring out of the gumball machine?" Jade said. "Welp, that's the best we can do with it."

"HAHAHAHAHA! You're joking?! My mom used to give me quarters for that machine when I was little. I thought the stuff in there was questionable. And you know what? The only places that still have those things are malls and old arcades." I said, amused.

When the lights returned to the original color I noticed a presence behind us. I spun around and found a gang of fair-hes dressed in all black with black sunglasses staring at us. These weren't regular fair-hes. In fact, these must have been the guards.

"The child alarm was set off in this area, Tony," the guard in front said angrily. "You wouldn't happen to know anything about that would you?" The mouthguard leaned down and right up to Tony's face.

My hand was still in the air to say hello, forgetting that me being here was basically illegal, when Tony and the jewel-hers said, "No, sir."

As the guard's eyes looked us over, one of them pointed to my dang pajamas sticking out from under my pant leg. Tony's eyes followed theirs and he shouted, "RUN!"

CHAPTER 8

THE CHASE

---- * ☆ 🦷 ☆ * ----

Before my brain could process what was said, my feet were moving. But where the heck was I supposed to go? At that moment, while running down a long hall with really slippery yet shiny floors, I realized that Tony may be a little bit of a rebel. Why had the mouthguard assumed Tony was behind the kid alarm going off? And why do they have a kid alarm? Does that mean I'm not the first kid here?! But no one has ever made it back? This is it. This is how it ends.

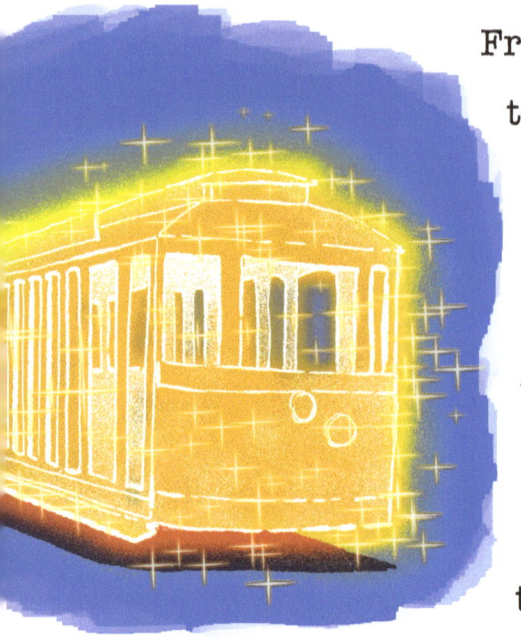

Frantically looking for a place to hide, I leapt into a parked trolley of dust. I was trying to calm my heavy breathing but I could still hear chaos whirling all around me. Tony was buzzing around like he was caught between third and home base with guards on both sides. Ok, he was toying with these guys. But these ninja-like mouthguards weren't giving up. The jewel-hers kept trying to distract them by throwing glittering dust balls at each of the guards. But they flew and ran so fast, switching from wing to foot speed and back. The glitter balls exploded as they made contact and it looked like the fourth of July in here.

Gemma, Jade, and Diamond got cornered on the opposite end of the room from where I was still hiding, by five or six ninja guards. I couldn't make out everything being said but I did hear the guard as he chased Tony closer to my hiding spot.

"This is the last straw, Tony. The Grand Fair-He has no more tolerance for your games. We have lost a lot of good fairies because of you." He now had Tony cornered. I could see my tooth fair-he struggling but didn't know how I could help, or even if I should.

And what did they mean by that? Crouching lower into the trolley, I could hear Tony's muffled voice pleading that none of what had happened before was his fault. He added that tonight he was trying to earn his compassion badge to move up in his fair-he career. There is clearly so much I still do not know.

"We can't just rely on kids believing in us without spreading a little wonder. It's the mystery of it all that keeps this whirlpool whirling. I mean, come on guys, how do you think Santa keeps his magic flowing?" I heard Tony yell.

"It's dangerous! The last thing we need are these politicians and government systems taking our fairhes to Area 51 like some one-eyed green gremlin!" the mouthguard replied.

They continued walking side by side more like friends than like the enemies I thought they were. As the two of them went back and forth, the sounds got further away until they exited the room and everything was quiet. I waited for a moment then figured I should get out of this trolley when I heard footsteps coming right for my side of the trolley. Oh no, this is it, I thought. I'd ruined Tony's career and I'd never get any money again for any of my amazing teeth. But the worst part was that I knew I'd never get back home to my family or my PlayStation! Forever naughty listed.

As emotions started taking over, I forced myself to hold back tears. In doing, some of the dust tickled my nose and I had to try hard not to sneeze. I knew one of those mouthguards was super close, but the dust was so thick I couldn't help it. "AH CHOO!" I froze.

The footsteps stopped and my heart was beating so loud I'm positive anyone within a mile radius heard it. To my surprise, Tony popped over the side of the trolley. "It's you?" I said with relief. "But I

thought those mouthguard ninja people captured you?"

Tony leaned over the edge of the cart, "Oh, that? That was my cousin. We are good, but we do need to get you out of here."

"I could have sworn that it was someone else getting closer to me," I said. "Glitch magic," Tony said matter of factly. "It was a guard but I knew he was there and switched places with him. It's one of my specialty tricks."

CHAPTER 9

THE RETURN

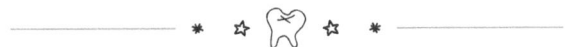

From the windows ahead, I could tell the sun was starting to rise. How can this place look more beautiful and glow any brighter? Who knows, but it was happening.

Tony looked over to the windows and for the first time tonight, I saw a hint of fear in his eyes. This was bad on so many levels.

"Kid! Let's get you home, now!!" he shouted. Tony snatched me up by my fake wings and out of the dusty trolley. "Do you have your Air Fair-Hes laced up tight?" he asked.

"Uh, yeah, I think so," I replied, looking down at my feet.

"All right, click your heels together three times."

"What? No way!"

Tony laughed under his breath before he put his hand on my shoulder. "Kid, I'm kidding. But the look on your face was pretty priceless."

How was he joking at a time like this?!

"You want to know another secret?" Tony leaned in. I nodded quickly and noticed the morning sunlight beginning to approach. "Our shoes help store fair-he magic. The jewel-hers' magic is stored in their jewels and the mouthguards' in their masks. Without Air Fair-Hes, tooth fair-hes can't get everywhere we need to be in one night. The elves have their snapbacks and the sleigh and we have these." He continued, "You know what? Better idea. Let's swap shoes. With mine, you should have enough magic to fly home next to me and I should have enough in me to get to your place and back." We quickly swapped left shoe for left shoe and right for right. "Ok. We don't have much time. Just trust me here. Stomp your right foot twice and be ready."

I looked at my shoes then back up to Tony. He stomped twice and shot right up into the sky. "Well, here goes nothing," and as soon as my foot hit the floor the second time, I went flying. I was super wobbly at first but as I followed Tony through the castle and out the massive gates, we went higher into the sky. I couldn't help but put my arms up like superman like I'd seen Tony do when we flew here. It didn't just look cool, but it helped to keep me balanced.

"Relax your arms!" Tony shouted. "You can go faster or slower by pointing or flexing your feet. Just use your arms to guide and balance yourself," Tony told me as he was struggling to keep up with my flailing flying body. Apparently I wasn't catching on as fast as I thought. I tried to do what he said and

started to get my bearings. "There ya go kid, you got it!" He cheered me on. "You're a natural!"

"This is awesome! Really and extremely way too high, but so awesome!" I quickly felt more comfortable and was flying in circles around Tony.

"The first time is always the best! But look," He trailed off.

A mouthguard was suddenly at our sides.

Oh no, not again!

"It's getting late. Well, early. You know what I mean. We need to make sure you get home safe," the mouthguard said to me.

I don't remember seeing him before. He looked like he had more drip than the rest of them. It took me a minute to spot the difference. How did I not notice immediately his Air Fair-Hes were all black? My dad said anyone with all black shoes was dangerous according to comics he read growing up. And that did prove true with all those mouthguards earlier. I think this guy is safe though. I think.

I saw him and Tony dap up mid-flight, so it's confirmed: he's a good mouthguard.

"Look Tony, I sent them in the wrong direction but my team is elite. It won't take them long. I can't get you out of trouble again. Dad is going to make an example of you if he catches you doing all of this. He is the Grand Fair-He and all!"

"I know, I know. How could I forget?" Tony mumbled.

"If you don't respect his rules, how is he supposed to expect other people to respect them?" the mystery guard started.

But hold up, HIS DAD?! Tony was like the prince of freaking Wakanda and he had me hiding in coal carts and running for my life? Tony nodded and fist bumped the guy who slowed his pace and turned back towards the canal.

"Okay, Gabe!" Tony refocused and pointed up to the slowly fading stars that were shifting in the sky like they had when we arrived. "We will fly right through the two front teeth. When you pop out the other side, you will know exactly where you are. I'm right here with you."

Tony glanced back at the guard who had stopped to watch and, I guess, make sure we really would leave. Tony and I both gave him a head nod and he nodded back.

He kept watch over our exit as we tried to beat the rising sun behind him.

Tony sped up and I followed as best I could. We were flying right at the stars. They got bigger and brighter the closer we got. Before I knew it, we were passing through. He was right, too, because when we crossed the gap in the stars, we were right above my house. "Glitch magic?" I questioned.

"Glitch magic," he confirmed. "All right, now slow it down. Remember, you gotta flex your feet a bit. That's it."

"I don't know about this. I'm going to fall," I cried.

"Well, only a little. You got it!" he said. I watched him hit a superhero landing and when I tried to do it too, it was more like a super loser landing…again! Flump! I landed right on my cheeks -- and not the ones your grandma pinched when you went to visit.

We both laughed as Tony helped me up and brushed me off. That's when I realized we were still tiny. We stood there on my windowsill watching the sun come up.

"All right, listen closely. We have to hurry," Tony grabbed my shoulders and turned me so we were facing each other. "Stomp your left foot once and think about where you want to go -- inside your room. That is where you will appear. Then when you take those shoes off, you will turn back into your regular size self." He paused waiting for me to follow his instructions. "Do it now!"

CHAPTER 10

BACK TO REALITY... MAYBE

I swallowed, closed my eyes, took a deep breath and stomped my left foot. By the time I finished exhaling, I was standing on my bedpost looking at Tony back on the outside windowsill. He pointed to my shoes and motioned, reminding me to take them off. I stepped out of one and then pulled the other off. As soon as both shoes were off, I fell from my bedpost onto my bed. I was big again. Well, regular size, still on the short side.

Tap, tap, tap.

I looked back over and saw tiny Tony do a step-back shot and heard the faintest, "Kobe!" He waited a moment then pointed to my pillow. I lifted it up and found a $5 bill. My tooth was a good one! Grabbing the money, I smiled and turned back around but Tony was gone.

"No, no, no!" I moaned as I hopped off my bed and ran to the window. I looked around frantically in each direction, but saw nothing. He was gone.

I never got to ask where they got the money from. But, I guess I did find out. The jewel-hers said

Santa's elves delivered the teeth to the stores! They must get money from each sale. Then give some to the kids when they pick up their teeth. I almost laughed out loud at the thought of elves zipping through the sky with Santa's red bag full of money.

"Honey, are you ok?" Oh no, mom was coming. I quickly climbed back into the bed and pulled my sheets up to my face.

I felt myself starting to get emotional, but I didn't know why. I was happy, but I was also sad the adventure was over. Who would ever believe me? Would I believe me? Would you believe me?

"Oh Gabe, are you all right? Did the tooth fairy trap not work?" she asked as she sat next to me on my bed.

"Fair-he," I quietly corrected.

"Hmm?" My mom pulled the covers down to uncover my face as she always does. And I felt her ring against my face like I always do. I grabbed her

hand. I swear her diamond sparkled a little extra tonight.

"Where did these come from?" Mom asked as she pulled her hand away and reached down to pick up the Air Fair-hes.

"No. Freaking. Way."

"Gabriel! Watch your mouth!" she said sternly.

"Sorry, mom. Uhh, a friend of mine gave them to me." I took them back and put them on the far side of my bed.

"I'm sorry your trap didn't work. I know you and dad worked hard at it. It's time for school." She double patted the bed. "Get up and get ready," she said while walking out of my room.

"Yeah, ok Mom. I'll be down in a few."

As soon as she was out of sight, I rolled onto the floor beside my bed. I grabbed the shoes and stared. I had a lot of questions that had been answered, but still had so many more. And even more new questions. Did Tony show me what happens to the teeth in hopes that I would never stop believing and he would never fade? He didn't seem upset when I said I was going to tell my friends. As a matter of fact-everything Tony did when I was with him seemed to be somewhat...on purpose?

"Hmm, I wonder," I said as I slipped my feet back into my new shoes.